GO QUIZ
YOURSELF!

HUMAN
BODY

IZZI HOWELL

90710 000 467 014

First published in Great Britain in 2020 by Wayland

Copyright © Hodder and Stoughton Limited, 2020

Produced for Wayland by
White-Thomson Publishing Ltd
www.wtpub.co.uk

All rights reserved.

Series Editor: Izzi Howell
Series Designer: Rocket Design (East Anglia) Ltd

HB ISBN: 978 1 5263 1282 2
PB ISBN: 978 1 5263 1283 9

LONDON BOROUGH OF RICHMOND UPON THAMES	
90710 000 467 014	
Askews & Holts	24-Mar-2021
J612 HOW JUNIOR NON-F	
RTHAH	

Wayland
An imprint of
Hachette Children's Group
Part of Hodder & Stoughton
Carmelite House
50 Victoria Embankment
London EC4Y 0DZ

An Hachette UK Company
www.hachette.co.uk
www.hachettechildrens.co.uk

Printed in Dubai

Picture acknowledgements:
Getty: switchpipipi 20, Graphic_BKK1979 33t, Tribalium 43c; Shutterstock: Jane Kelly, Olga Bolbot. Iconic Bestiary and DarkestBlue cover and title page, Macrovector 4, Lucia Fox 5t, VectorMine 5b, 12, 18r, 19b, 27tl, 36, 37t and 38, Olga Bolbot 6, Oleksandr Malysh 7t, Designua 7b, 18l, 19t, 37b and 39t, Vecton 8, Skalapendra 9t, EgudinKa 9c, Shanvood 9b, reuse from pages 4–9 10–11, GraphicsRF 13t, Aldona Griskeviciene 13b, Taleseedum 14, corbac40 15tl, peiyang 15tr, ShadeDesign 15b, reuse from pages 12–15 16–17, shopplaywood 21t, Illusart 21c, graphic-line 21b, reuse from pages 18–21 22–23, metamorworks 24t, Iconic Bestiary 24b, Aldona Griskeviciene 25t, Lemberg Vector studio 25c, Rost9 25b, Marochkina Anastasiia 26t, MatoomMi 26b, Panimoni 27tr, mei yanotai 27b, reuse from pages 24–27 28–29, Olga Bolbot 30t, Tefi 30c, john dory 30–31b, svtdesign 32t, gritsalak karalak 32b, Evellean 33b, reuse from pages 30–33 34–35, gritsalak karalak 39c, GoodStudio 39b, reuse from pages 36–39 40–41, solar22 42t, Nadya_Art 42c, Vasilyeva Larisa 42b, MicroOne 43t, Blan-k 43b, reuse from whole book 46–47. All design elements from Shutterstock.

Every effort has been made to clear copyright. Should there be any inadvertent omission, please apply to the publisher for rectification.

The website addresses (URLs) included in this book were valid at the time of going to press. However, it is possible that contents or addresses may have changed since the publication of this book. No responsibility for any such changes can be accepted by either the author or the publisher.

All facts and statistics were true at the time of print.

CONTENTS

HOW TO USE THIS BOOK

This book is packed full of amazing facts and statistics. When you've finished reading a section, test yourself with questions on the following page. Check your answers on pages 44–45 and see if you're a quizmaster or if you need to quiz it again! When you've finished, test your friends and family to find out who's the ultimate quiz champion!

OUR BODIES

The human body is incredibly complex. It is made up of hundreds of different parts, including organs, blood vessels, bones, nerves and muscles. All of these parts work together to keep us alive and healthy.

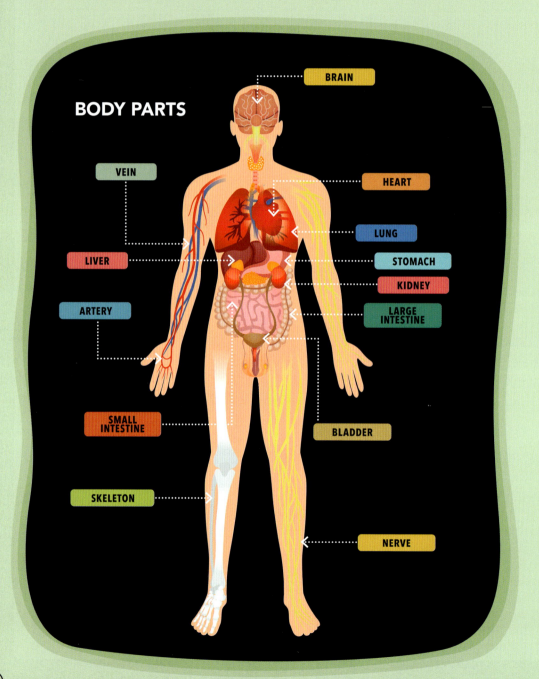

BODY PARTS

BRAIN

VEIN

HEART

LIVER

LUNG

STOMACH

KIDNEY

ARTERY

LARGE INTESTINE

SMALL INTESTINE

BLADDER

SKELETON

NERVE

ORGANS

The lungs and small intestine are both examples of organs. These are body parts with a specific function. For example, the lungs absorb oxygen while the small intestine absorbs nutrients from food. Most organs are inside the chest and head.

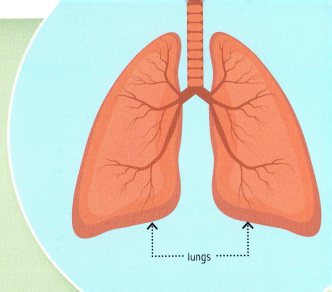

lungs

BODY TISSUES

The body is made up of different tissues, or materials. The skeleton is made of bone, which is a hard material made of minerals. Fat is a soft tissue stored in layers under the skin. Muscles are flexible tissues. The arms and legs are mostly made up of these different tissues.

FLUIDS

70 per cent of the body is made up of water, which is found in blood and in cells. Other fluids produced by the body include sweat and digestive juices from the stomach.

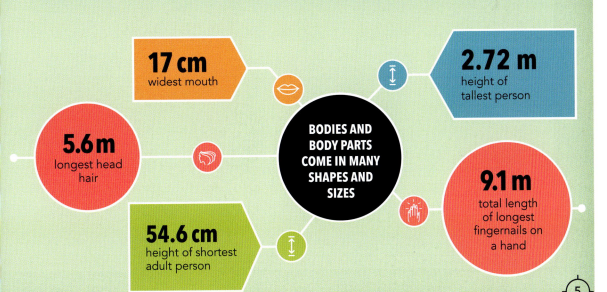

17 cm
widest mouth

2.72 m
height of tallest person

5.6 m
longest head hair

BODIES AND BODY PARTS COME IN MANY SHAPES AND SIZES

9.1 m
total length of longest fingernails on a hand

54.6 cm
height of shortest adult person

THE SKELETON

The skeleton provides support for the body and protects the organs. It also allows the body to move. The bones in the skeleton contain bone marrow, which produces red and white blood cells.

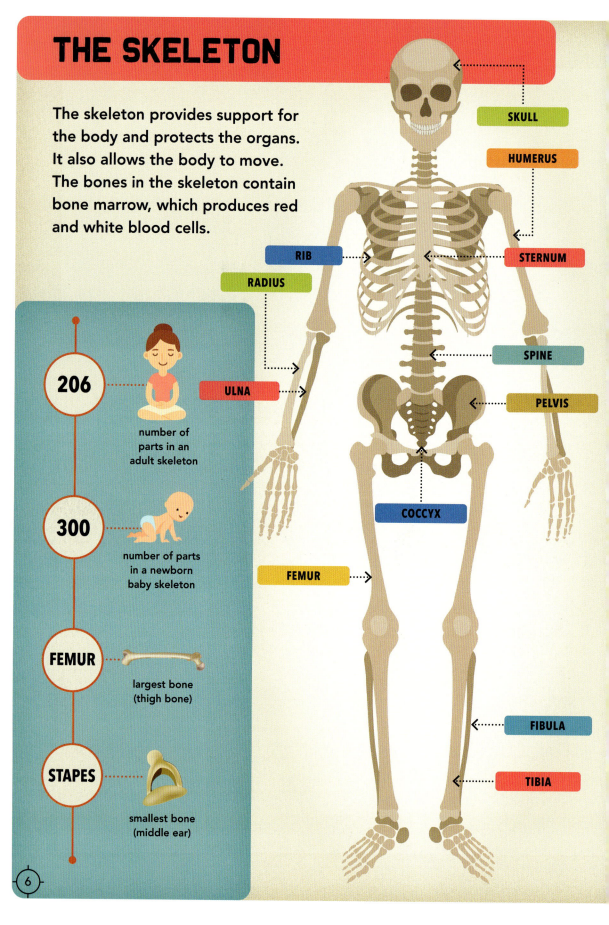

SKULL

HUMERUS

STERNUM

RIB

RADIUS

SPINE

ULNA

PELVIS

COCCYX

FEMUR

FIBULA

TIBIA

206 number of parts in an adult skeleton

300 number of parts in a newborn baby skeleton

FEMUR largest bone (thigh bone)

STAPES smallest bone (middle ear)

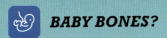

BABY BONES?

The skeleton of a baby has more parts than that of an adult! Babies' skeletons are mostly made of a soft material called cartilage, which is more flexible than bone. This makes it easier for the baby to be born. Over time, the cartilage turns to bone and some of the smaller parts join together into larger bones. This reduces the number of bones in the body.

AXIAL AND APPENDICULAR

The skeleton can be divided into two main parts – the axial skeleton and the appendicular skeleton. The axial skeleton is made up of the skull, spine and ribs.

The appendicular skeleton is made up of parts that come off the axial skeleton, such as the shoulders, arms, pelvis and legs.

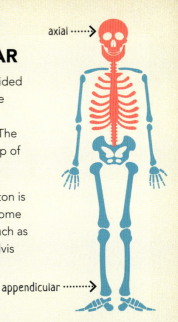

axial ······>

appendicular ········>

INSIDE A BONE

There are two types of bone: spongy and compact. Long bones are usually made of compact bone, while short bones are made of spongy bone.

Bone marrow is found inside long bones. Red bone marrow produces white and red blood cells, while yellow bone marrow stores fat.

Bones contain nerves and blood vessels.

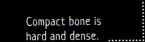

Compact bone is hard and dense. ··········

Spongy bone is lightweight. It is made up of a mesh with lots of gaps within it. ··········

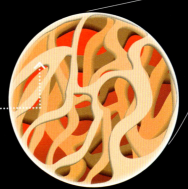

The outer layer of all bones is made of compact bone.

MUSCLES

Every movement requires muscles, from running and jumping to small actions such as swallowing or blinking. Muscles are also responsible for other processes that we aren't always aware of, such as digestion. There are three types of muscle in the body: skeletal, smooth and cardiac.

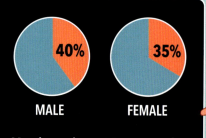

MALE 40%

FEMALE 35%

Muscles make up 40 per cent of an adult male's weight and 35 per cent of an adult female's weight.

MUSCLES AND BONES

Skeletal muscle is attached to bones with bands of tissue called tendons. These muscles control the movement of the body. This movement is voluntary – we choose which part of the body we want to move.

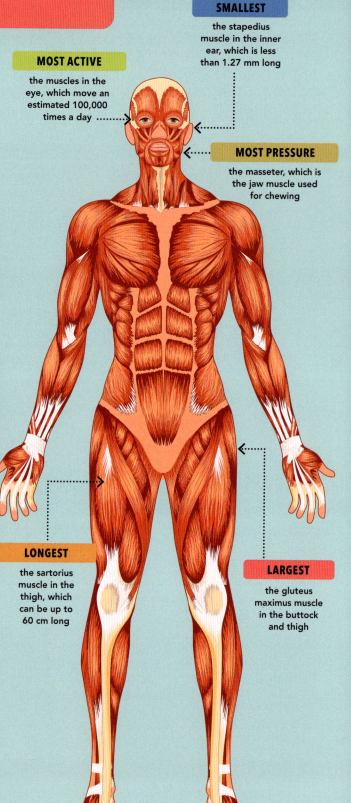

SMALLEST
the stapedius muscle in the inner ear, which is less than 1.27 mm long

MOST ACTIVE
the muscles in the eye, which move an estimated 100,000 times a day

MOST PRESSURE
the masseter, which is the jaw muscle used for chewing

LONGEST
the sartorius muscle in the thigh, which can be up to 60 cm long

LARGEST
the gluteus maximus muscle in the buttock and thigh

PULL AND RELAX

Muscles create movement by contracting (shortening). This makes the muscle pull.

Muscles often work in pairs, with one muscle contracting while the other relaxes. Most of the muscles in the arms and legs work in pairs.

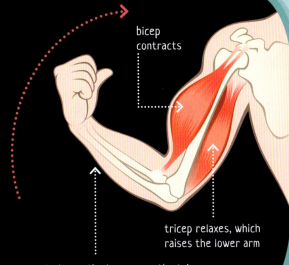

bicep contracts

tricep relaxes, which raises the lower arm

to lower the lower arm, the tricep contracts and the bicep relaxes

ORGAN MUSCLES

Smooth muscle is found in the walls of blood vessels and certain organs, such as the stomach and bladder. This muscle helps with different processes in these organs. For example, the contraction of muscles in the stomach helps to break down food for digestion. The movement of these muscles is involuntary.

stomach

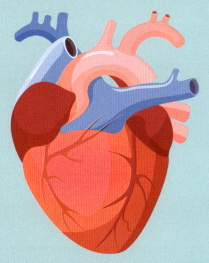

IN THE HEART

Cardiac muscle is found in the heart. These muscles contract to pump blood around the body (see pages 14–15). We can't control these muscles.

GO QUIZ YOURSELF!

1. What kind of body part is the small intestine?

2. Where are most organs found?

3. What percentage of the body is water?

4. What height was the shortest adult person?

5. What length was the longest head hair?

6. How many parts are there in an adult skeleton?

7. What is the largest bone?

8. Which parts is the axial skeleton made up of?

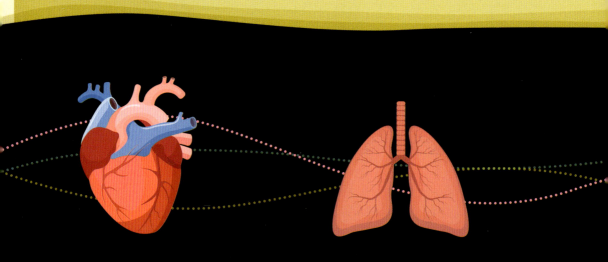

------→ **9** Which type of bone is the outer layer of all bone made of?

10 Which part of the bone produces red and white blood cells?

11 What are the three types of muscle?

12 What connects skeletal muscles to bones?

13 How long is the sartorius muscle, the longest muscle in the body?

14 Where are the most active muscles in the body found?

15 When one muscle in a pair contracts, what happens to the other muscle in the pair?

16 What type of muscle is found in the walls of blood vessels?

17 Where is cardiac muscle found?

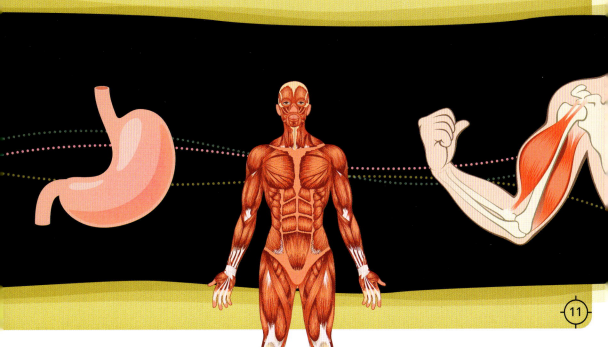

BREATHING AND LUNGS

Cells in the body need oxygen to work properly. The respiratory system takes air into the body and extracts oxygen for cells to use.

MOUTH, WINDPIPE, LUNGS

The respiratory system is made up of the mouth, nose, windpipe and lungs. When you breathe in, air containing oxygen enters the body. When you breathe out, waste gases, such as carbon dioxide, leave the body.

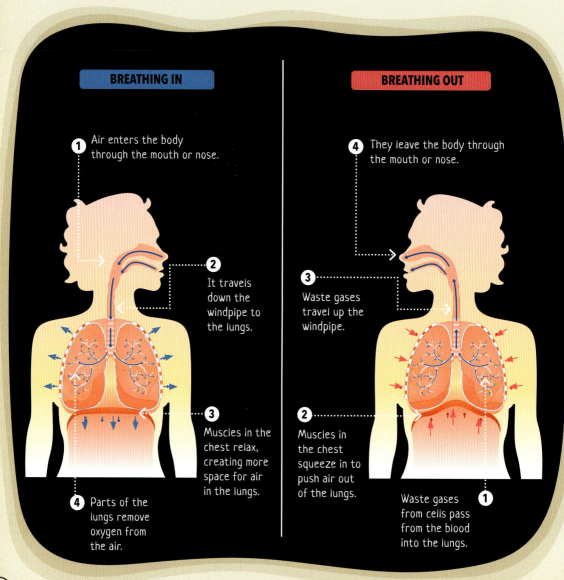

BREATHING IN

1 Air enters the body through the mouth or nose.

2 It travels down the windpipe to the lungs.

3 Muscles in the chest relax, creating more space for air in the lungs.

4 Parts of the lungs remove oxygen from the air.

BREATHING OUT

4 They leave the body through the mouth or nose.

3 Waste gases travel up the windpipe.

2 Muscles in the chest squeeze in to push air out of the lungs.

1 Waste gases from cells pass from the blood into the lungs.

INSIDE THE LUNGS

In the lungs, the windpipe splits into two large tubes called bronchi (singular bronchus). Each bronchus then splits into around 30,000 smaller tubes, called bronchioles. At the ends of the bronchioles are tiny air sacs called alveoli (singular alveolus).

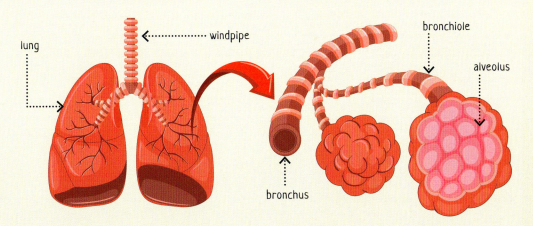

lung

windpipe

bronchiole

alveolus

bronchus

GAS EXCHANGE

Each alveolus is surrounded by blood vessels. This is where gas exchange takes place. The walls of the alveoli are very thin, so gas can pass through. Oxygen from air in the lungs enters the blood. Carbon dioxide and other waste gases are removed from the blood and pass back into the lungs.

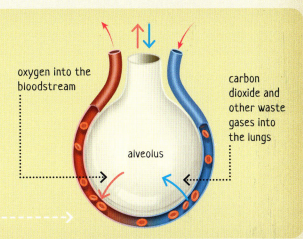

oxygen into the bloodstream

carbon dioxide and other waste gases into the lungs

alveolus

2,414 KM
the average total length of the airways in the lungs – that's half the distance between New York and Los Angeles!

8,000–9,000 LITRES
the amount of air we breathe in every day

LUNG FACTS

17,000 approximate number of breaths we take every day

600 MILLION
approximate number of alveoli in an adult's lungs

THE HEART AND BLOOD

The heart pumps blood around the body. Blood carries oxygen and nutrients to the cells. It also transports other useful substances around the body, such as hormones.

THE HEART

The heart is a muscle around the size of a fist. It pumps blood by contracting and relaxing. This squeezes blood through the heart.

HALVES OF THE HEART

The heart is divided into two halves. In the left side of the heart, oxygen-rich blood from the lungs is pumped to the rest of the body. In the right side of the heart, used blood from the body is pumped to the lungs. There, carbon dioxide is removed. Each half of the heart has two chambers, known as the atrium and the ventricle.

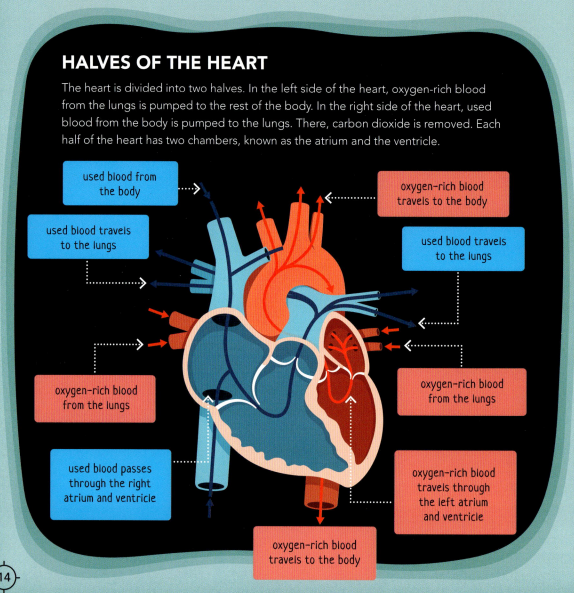

used blood from the body

used blood travels to the lungs

oxygen-rich blood from the lungs

used blood passes through the right atrium and ventricle

oxygen-rich blood travels to the body

oxygen-rich blood travels to the body

used blood travels to the lungs

oxygen-rich blood from the lungs

oxygen-rich blood travels through the left atrium and ventricle

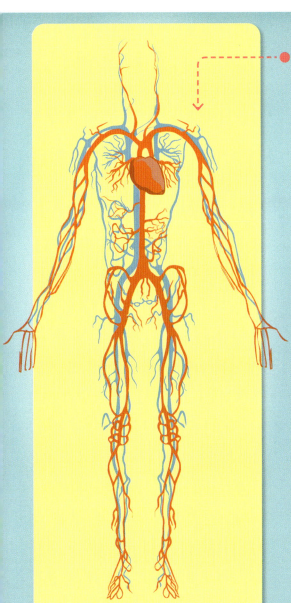

BLOOD VESSELS

There are two main types of blood vessel: veins and arteries. Arteries carry blood from the heart to the body, while veins carry blood from the body back to the heart.

Arteries and veins are connected by tiny blood vessels called capillaries.

 VERY LONG VESSELS

If an adult's blood vessels were laid out end to end, the distance would be enough to circle Earth's equator four times!

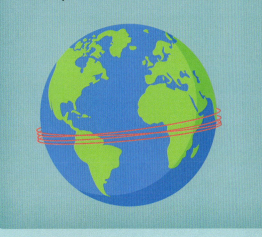

BLOOD

The main ingredients of blood are plasma, red blood cells, white blood cells and platelets. Plasma is a liquid, which is mainly made up of water. Red blood cells carry oxygen around the body. Waste chemicals and hormones, which give instructions to different parts of the body, are also transported in blood. White blood cells are an important part of the immune system (see pages 32–33). Platelets help with blood clotting.

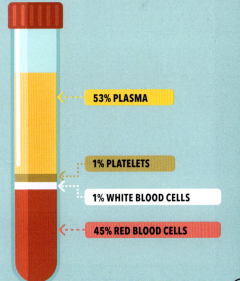

53% PLASMA

1% PLATELETS

1% WHITE BLOOD CELLS

45% RED BLOOD CELLS

GO QUIZ YOURSELF!

18 Which body parts make up the respiratory system?

19 What leaves the body when you breathe out?

20 Why do muscles in the chest relax when you breathe in?

21 How many bronchioles does each bronchus split into?

22 What is an alveolus?

23 Why are the walls of the alveoli very thin?

24 How many litres of air do we breathe in every day?

25 How long are the airways in the lungs?

26 Approximately how many breaths do we take every day?

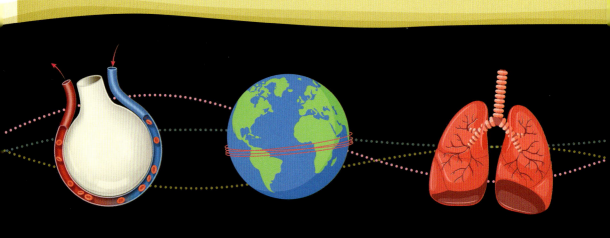

27 In which half of the heart is oxygen-rich blood from the lungs pumped to the rest of the body?

28 What are the names of the two chambers in each half of the heart?

29 What is an artery?

30 What is the name for a tiny blood vessel that connects an artery and a vein?

31 What do red blood cells do?

32 As well as oxygen, which other substances are carried around the body by blood?

33 Which ingredient in blood helps with blood clotting?

34 What percentage of blood is made up of red blood cells?

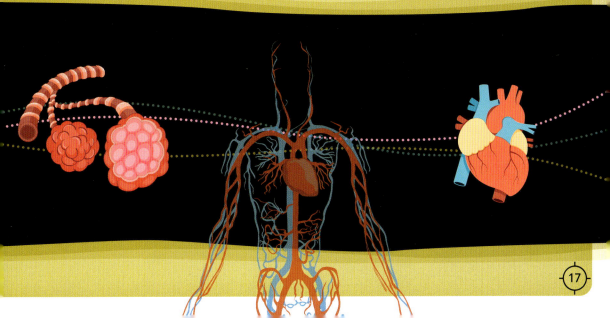

THE NERVOUS SYSTEM

The nervous system is made up of a network of nerves, which runs across the body. It also includes the brain and the spinal cord. Nerve cells carry electrical messages around the body and to and from the brain.

NERVES AND NEURONES

Nerves are bundles of neurones (nerve cells). There are three different types of neurone.

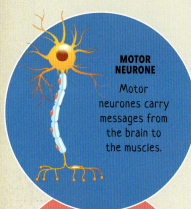

MOTOR NEURONE

Motor neurones carry messages from the brain to the muscles.

SENSORY NEURONE

Sensory neurones collect information from sensory organs, such as the eyes.

RELAY NEURONE

Relay neurones connect sensory and motor neurones.

NERVES IN THE BODY

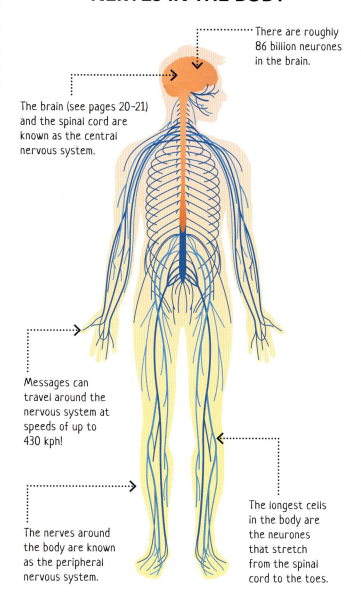

There are roughly 86 billion neurones in the brain.

The brain (see pages 20–21) and the spinal cord are known as the central nervous system.

Messages can travel around the nervous system at speeds of up to 430 kph!

The nerves around the body are known as the peripheral nervous system.

The longest cells in the body are the neurones that stretch from the spinal cord to the toes.

PASSING IT ON

Messages travel very quickly along neurones and around the nervous system. There are actually very small gaps between neurones. These are called synapses. Chemicals in the synapse carry the message across the gap from one neurone to the next.

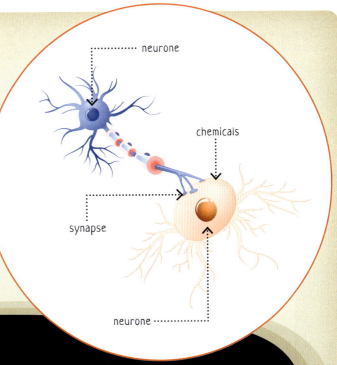

neurone

chemicals

synapse

neurone

REFLEXES

Sometimes, the body automatically reacts without receiving instructions from the brain. This is known as a reflex reaction. These reactions keep us safe from danger, such as high temperatures or pain. They are much faster than standard reactions, as they don't have to come via the brain, so we are protected sooner.

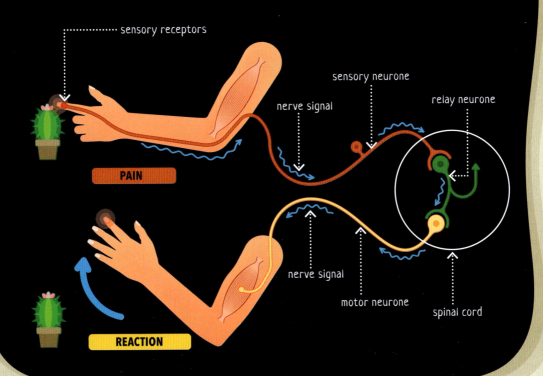

sensory receptors

sensory neurone

relay neurone

nerve signal

PAIN

nerve signal

motor neurone

spinal cord

REACTION

THE BRAIN

The brain is the control centre of the body. It controls our movement, feelings and thoughts, as well as many unconscious actions, such as digestion and breathing.

● THE PARTS OF THE BRAIN

CEREBRUM

The cerebrum is the biggest part of the brain. Its wrinkles give it extra surface area for neurones. It is split into two halves. This part of the brain controls speech, feelings and conscious actions.

CORPUS CALLOSUM

The corpus callosum connects the two parts of the cerebrum.

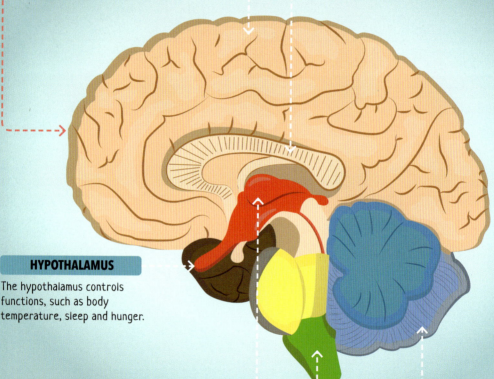

HYPOTHALAMUS

The hypothalamus controls functions, such as body temperature, sleep and hunger.

THALAMUS

The thalamus processes signals from the senses and sends them to other parts of the brain.

BRAINSTEM

The brainstem connects the brain to the spinal cord and the nervous system. It controls many involuntary processes, such as the heartbeat.

CEREBELLUM

The cerebellum is located under the cerebrum. It controls movement and balance.

LOBES

Each half, or hemisphere of the cerebrum, is divided into four main sections, known as lobes. The four lobes are the frontal lobe, the parietal lobe, the temporal lobe and the occipital lobe. The neurones in each lobe control different functions. Some functions are controlled by more than one lobe.

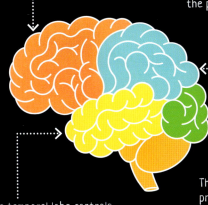

The frontal lobe controls voluntary movement, planning and short-term memory.

The parietal lobe processes language and information about touch, and controls balance and the position of the body.

The temporal lobe controls memory and helps us to understand language.

The occipital lobe processes information from the eyes.

THINKING AND REMEMBERING

When we think, electrical signals travel around the brain along neurones. Thanks to these cells, we think about real situations, imaginary ideas or remember things that happened in the past. We also have two types of memory. Short-term memory helps us to remember what we're doing at the current moment. Long-term memory helps us to remember information and details from further back in time.

LEARNING

The billions of neurones in the brain are connected to each other. When we learn new things, it strengthens these connections or even creates new connections. This is why it gets easier to do new things with practice, such as playing a musical instrument.

GO QUIZ YOURSELF!

35 What is a neurone?

36 What are the three types of neurone?

37 Which type of neurone carries messages from the brain to the muscles?

38 Which body parts make up the central nervous system?

39 Which neurones are the longest cells in the body?

40 How fast can messages travel around the nervous system?

41 Approximately how many neurones are there in the brain?

42 What happens at a synapse?

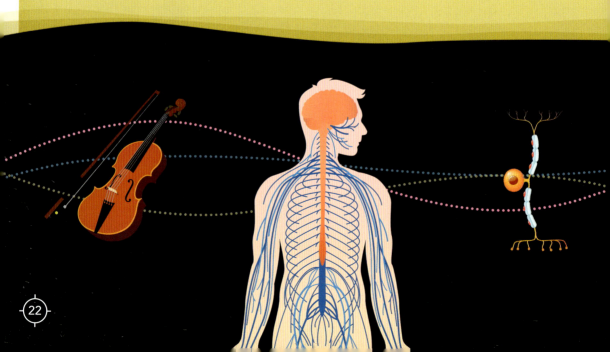

43 What is a reflex reaction?

44 What is the biggest part of the brain?

45 Which part of the brain connects the brain to the spinal cord and nervous system?

46 What does the hypothalamus do?

47 What are the four lobes found in each part of the cerebrum?

48 What is the role of the temporal lobe?

49 Which lobe processes information from the eyes?

50 What are the two types of memory?

51 Why do new tasks become easier with practice?

THE DIGESTIVE SYSTEM

The digestive system breaks down food so that the body can use it. Cells need energy from food to work properly. Other nutrients from food are also needed to repair cells and grow new ones.

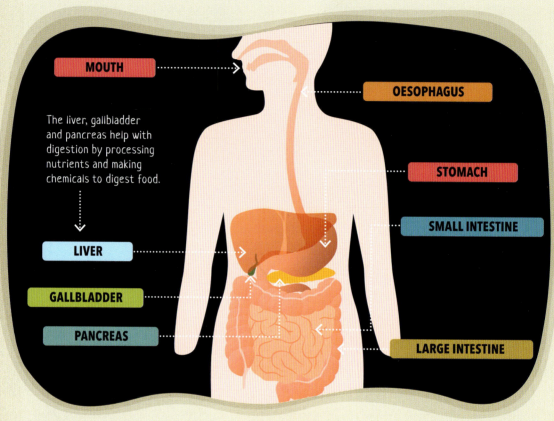

The liver, gallbladder and pancreas help with digestion by processing nutrients and making chemicals to digest food.

MOUTH

OESOPHAGUS

STOMACH

SMALL INTESTINE

LIVER

GALLBLADDER

PANCREAS

LARGE INTESTINE

IN THE MOUTH

Digestion begins in the mouth. The teeth cut, crush and grind food into smaller pieces. The mouth releases saliva (spit), which mixes with the broken-down food to make a paste. The tongue forms this paste into a ball (known as a bolus) and pushes it to the back of the mouth, ready to be swallowed.

SO MUCH SPIT!

We produce around one litre of saliva every day!

● SWALLOWING

When we swallow, the bolus is forced down the oesophagus. There is a flap at the back of the throat that covers the windpipe so that food doesn't accidentally go down into the lungs instead. Muscles in the walls of the oesophagus push the food down to the stomach, with the help of gravity.

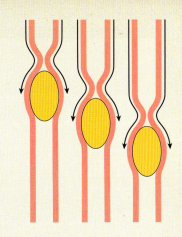

THE STOMACH

In the stomach, food is broken down further into a thick liquid called chyme. This is done in two ways. Muscles in the stomach wall contract to squeeze and churn the food. The stomach also releases gastric juices that contain acid and enzymes to break down the food.

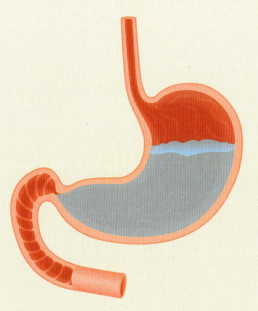

 HOW LONG?

The organs that make up the digestive system of an adult would measure around 9 m if they were laid out straight!

THE SMALL INTESTINE

The small intestine is lined with millions of tiny finger-shaped stalks, called villi. There are around 10 to 40 villi per square mm of the small intestine.

Each villus is around 0.5 to 1 mm long.

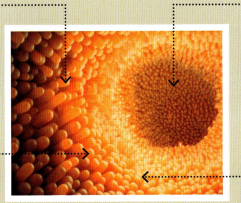

The villi absorb nutrients from broken-down food. These nutrients pass into the bloodstream through blood vessels in the villi.

Any undigested food that remains after passing through the small intestine travels through the large intestine (see page 26) before leaving the body.

REMOVING WASTE

Waste from the digestive system and other parts of the body is removed in faeces and urine. Each type of waste leaves the body in a different way.

THE LARGE INTESTINE

Most of the useful nutrients from the broken-down food that enters the large intestine have already been absorbed in the small intestine. Water and some vitamins are absorbed from this food in the large intestine. The rest dries out into solid lumps (faeces).

LEAVING THE BODY

Faeces move into the rectum when they are ready to leave the body. When you go to the toilet, faeces leave the body through an opening called the anus.

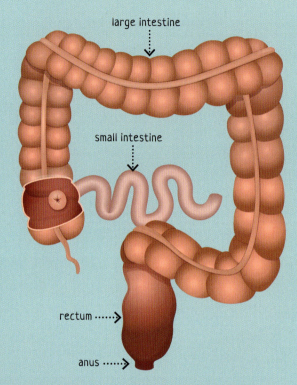

large intestine

small intestine

rectum ······>

anus ······>

THE URINARY SYSTEM

The urinary system is made up of the kidneys and the bladder. The kidneys filter the blood and remove waste from it. The clean blood continues to flow around the body.

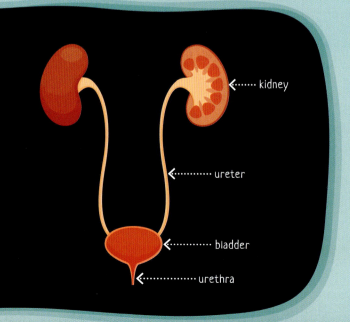

<······· kidney

<············ ureter

<············ bladder

<············ urethra

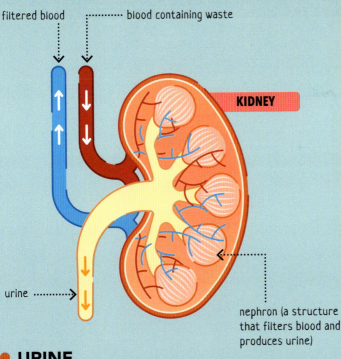

filtered blood

blood containing waste

KIDNEY

urine

nephron (a structure that filters blood and produces urine)

The kidneys filter all of the blood in the body every 45 minutes!

● URINE

In the kidneys, waste chemicals and water combine to form urine. This leaves the kidneys through the ureters, which are tubes that carry urine to the bladder. Urine is stored in the stretchy bladder. When the bladder is full, it sends a message to the brain so that we know to go to the toilet and release the urine.

The average length of an adult kidney is **10 cm**.

Each kidney contains **1 TO 1.25 MILLION** nephrons.

If your kidneys stop working, you can use a **DIALYSIS MACHINE** to clean your blood or receive a kidney transplant from someone else.

It is possible to survive with only **1 KIDNEY**.

GO QUIZ YOURSELF!

52 What is the role of the teeth in digestion?

53 Approximately how much saliva do we produce in a day?

54 What stops food from going down the windpipe when it is swallowed?

55 How do muscles in the oesophagus help food to reach the stomach?

56 What is chyme?

57 How do the stomach walls help with digestion?

58 How long is a villus?

59 How are nutrients absorbed by the villi in the small intestine?

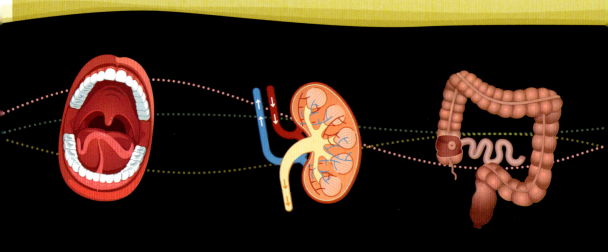

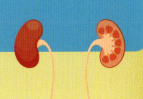

- - - - - - > **60** How long would the organs in the digestive system measure if they were laid out straight?

61 What is absorbed from broken-down food in the large intestine?

62 What are faeces?

63 Where do faeces move to when they are ready to leave the body?

64 What is the role of the kidneys?

65 On average, how long is an adult kidney?

66 How often do the kidneys filter all of the blood in the body?

67 What are the ureters?

68 Which waste product is stored in the bladder?

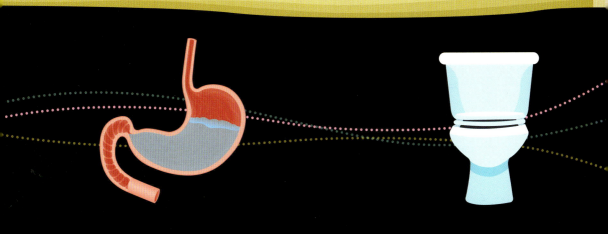

THE REPRODUCTIVE SYSTEM

The reproductive system is different in males and females. The male and female reproductive systems produce sex cells that, when joined together, can develop into a baby.

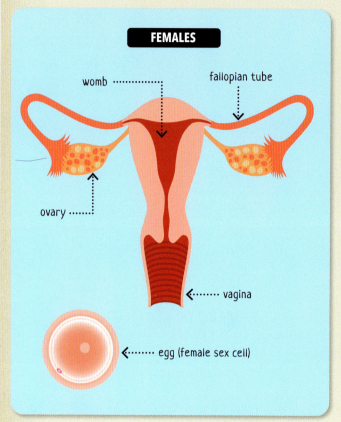

FEMALES

womb

fallopian tube

ovary

vagina

egg (female sex cell)

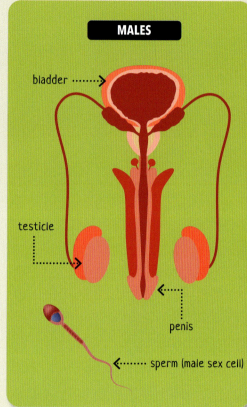

MALES

bladder

testicle

penis

sperm (male sex cell)

PREGNANCY

If a sperm cell meets an egg cell, the sperm can fertilise the egg. The fertilised egg sticks to the wall of the womb and starts dividing into new cells. These new cells develop into a baby in the womb. After around 40 weeks, the baby is born. Muscles in the walls of the womb contract to help push the baby out.

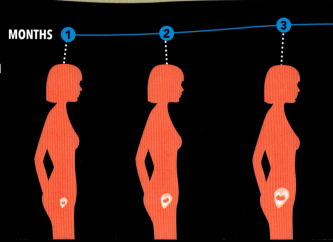

MONTHS   1   2   3

FEMALES

Eggs are produced in the ovaries. Once a month, an egg is released from an ovary and travels along a fallopian tube. If the egg is fertilised by a sperm, it can implant in the womb and develop into a baby (see below). If the egg is not fertilised, it remains in the womb until menstruation, when the womb lining is shed through the vagina.

MALES

Sperm are produced in the testicles. During sexual activity, sperm leave the body through the penis.

PUBERTY

During puberty, a child's body develops into the body of an adult and the reproductive system develops. Puberty is caused by hormones and usually happens during the teenage years.

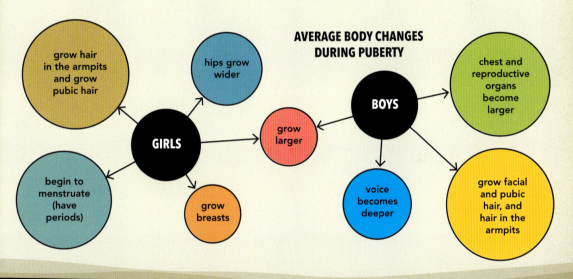

AVERAGE BODY CHANGES DURING PUBERTY

grow hair in the armpits and grow pubic hair

hips grow wider

chest and reproductive organs become larger

GIRLS

BOYS

grow larger

begin to menstruate (have periods)

grow breasts

voice becomes deeper

grow facial and pubic hair, and hair in the armpits

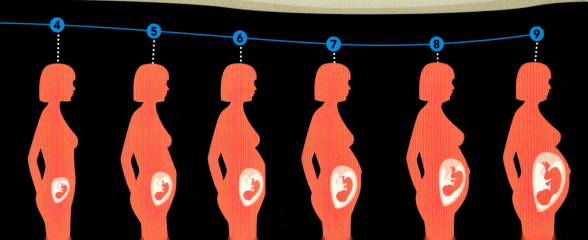

THE IMMUNE SYSTEM

Our immune system protects us against germs, which can cause disease if they enter the body. We can help boost our immune system by taking care of ourselves and getting vaccinated against diseases.

FIRST DEFENCES

The best way to keep healthy is to stop germs from getting inside the body. Our skin is a barrier that stops germs from getting into the bloodstream. Tiny hairs in the nose trap and block germs. Saliva in the mouth also contains chemicals that can kill some bacteria.

WHITE BLOOD CELLS

Germs can enter the bloodstream through cuts. White blood cells defend the body against germs in the blood. They surround and absorb the germs, breaking them down into small, harmless pieces. The white blood cells then return the pieces of germ back into the bloodstream. They will be filtered from the blood in the kidneys and released as waste.

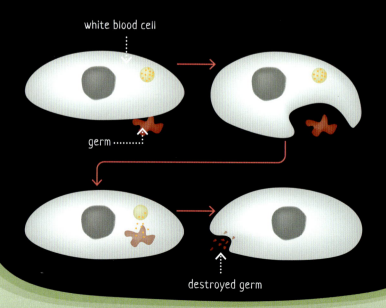

white blood cell

germ

destroyed germ

There are between

4,500 and 11,000

white blood cells in one cubic mm of blood from a healthy adult.

ANTIBODIES

Some white blood cells make antibodies, which are chemicals that attack germs. Antibodies fight specific types of germ by sticking on to them and making them useless. Once your body has been exposed to a germ, it learns how to make antibodies against it. If the same germ gets into the body again, the antibodies will be ready and waiting to fight it off again.

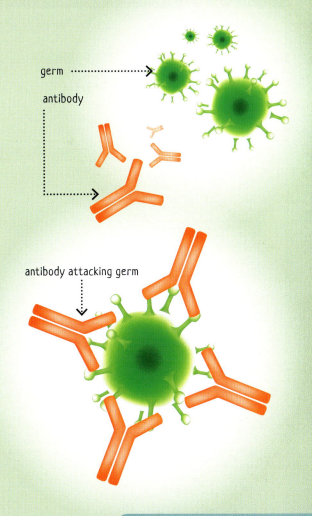

germ

antibody

antibody attacking germ

VACCINATIONS

Vaccinations are a way of protecting the body against certain germs. A vaccination is a weakened form of a germ that is introduced into the body so that white blood cells learn how to make the antibodies that protect against it without the body becoming ill. Then, if you are exposed to the real germ later, you will be protected as you already have the antibodies to fight against it.

GOING, GOING ...

Vaccinations have helped to greatly reduce cases of serious diseases, such as polio. One disease, smallpox, was entirely wiped out worldwide in 1980, thanks to vaccinations.

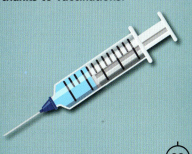

GO QUIZ YOURSELF!

69 Where are egg cells produced?

70 How often is an egg cell released?

71 What happens if an egg cell is not fertilised?

72 Where are sperm cells produced?

73 What happens during puberty?

74 When does puberty usually happen?

75 Name one feature of puberty in boys.

76 What happens to girls' hips during puberty?

77 In which body part does an unborn baby develop?

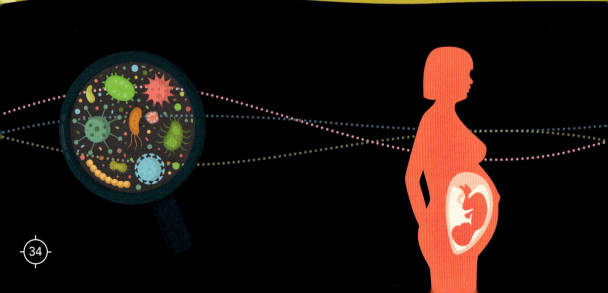

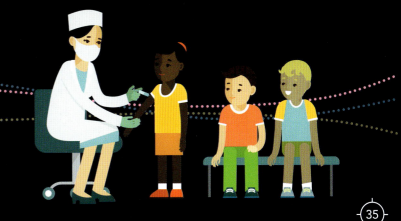

SEEING AND HEARING

We have five main senses: seeing, hearing, taste, touch and smell. We use these senses to understand the world around us.

TO THE BRAIN

Sense organs, such as the eye or the ear, send messages to the brain about the information they have gathered. These messages travel along nerves (see pages 18–19) to the brain, which interprets the information. The brain then responds by sending out messages to tell the body how to react to the sensory information, for example, by moving towards an object that was being looked for.

HEARING

The outer ear acts as a funnel for sound waves, guiding them into the part of the ear that is inside the head. Sound waves travel along the ear canal and hit the eardrum, which makes it vibrate. The vibrations travel through small bones in the inner ear and into the cochlea. Tiny hairs in the cochlea pick up the vibrations and convert them into a message that is sent to the brain.

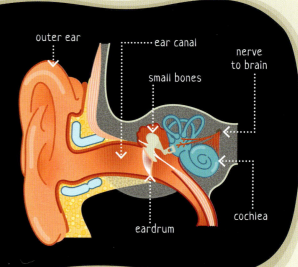

outer ear · ear canal · nerve to brain · small bones · eardrum · cochlea

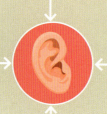

12 cm length of the longest earlobes. Earlobes never stop growing.

YOUNGER PEOPLE can hear high-pitched sounds that older people can't. This is because our hearing becomes damaged as we grow older.

The ears produce **EARWAX** to keep dirt and germs out. Too much earwax can result in hearing problems.

The brain can process words that we hear **WHILE WE ARE ASLEEP!**

SEEING

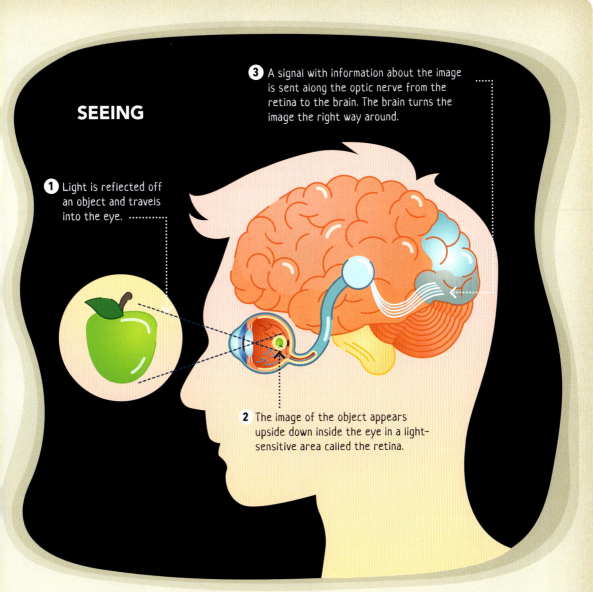

1 Light is reflected off an object and travels into the eye. ⋯⋯⋯⋯

3 A signal with information about the image is sent along the optic nerve from the retina to the brain. The brain turns the image the right way around.

2 The image of the object appears upside down inside the eye in a light-sensitive area called the retina.

RODS AND CONES

The retina contains special cells called rods and cones. Rod cells detect white light, while cone cells detect coloured light. They convert this light into electrical signals that go to the brain. There are around 130 million rods and 7 million cones in each eye.

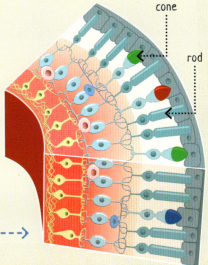

cone

rod

TOUCH, TASTE AND SMELL

We often think of seeing and hearing as the 'main' senses, but we actually get a huge amount of information from touching, smelling and tasting. As well as these five main senses, there are also other senses that are key to keeping us safe and informed.

TASTE

Tiny structures on the tongue called taste buds recognise flavour chemicals in the food that we eat and send messages about them to the brain. Our sense of taste allows us to enjoy delicious food, as well as keeping us safe from dangerous foods, such as rotten food, that often taste bad.

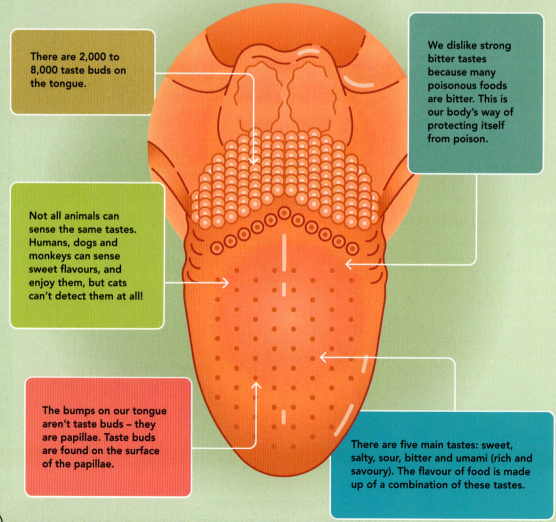

There are 2,000 to 8,000 taste buds on the tongue.

We dislike strong bitter tastes because many poisonous foods are bitter. This is our body's way of protecting itself from poison.

Not all animals can sense the same tastes. Humans, dogs and monkeys can sense sweet flavours, and enjoy them, but cats can't detect them at all!

The bumps on our tongue aren't taste buds – they are papillae. Taste buds are found on the surface of the papillae.

There are five main tastes: sweet, salty, sour, bitter and umami (rich and savoury). The flavour of food is made up of a combination of these tastes.

TOUCH

Sense receptors pick up different sensations, such as hot or cold temperatures, different textures and pain. There are many sense receptors in the skin, especially in sensitive places, such as the fingertips.

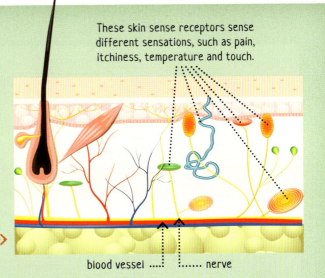

These skin sense receptors sense different sensations, such as pain, itchiness, temperature and touch.

blood vessel ..... : .... nerve

SMELL

Certain objects give off smell molecules, which float in the air and travel into the nose. Smell receptor cells inside the nose recognise the smells and pass on a message to the brain.

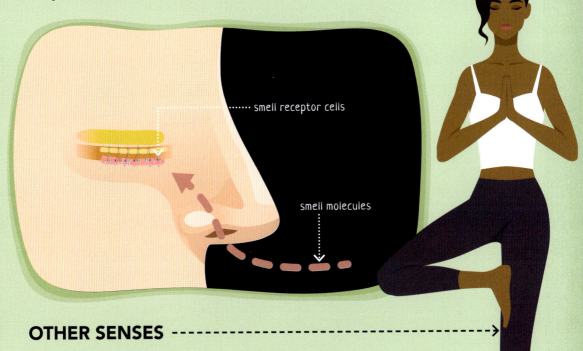

smell receptor cells

smell molecules

OTHER SENSES

We actually have more than just five senses. Our sense of balance stops us from falling over. Sensors in the ears track the position of the body. The brain sends messages to our body to change position and keep our balance if we are at risk of falling over. Proprioception is our sense of the position of the body and how it is moving. This helps us to understand our position in relation to other objects or the speed at which we are moving.

86 What are the five main senses?

87 Which nerve connects the retina and the brain?

88 In which part of the eye are rods and cones found?

89 Which type of cell detects coloured light?

90 Which part of the ear do sound waves hit first after travelling through the ear canal?

91 What happens in the cochlea?

92 Which part of the ear never stops growing?

93 Why do the ears produce earwax?

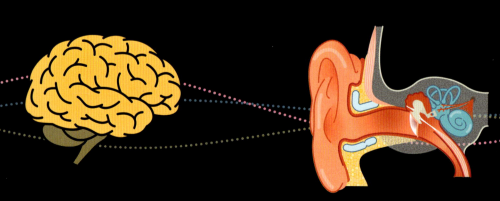

94 Which part of the tongue recognises flavour chemicals in food?

95 How does our sense of taste keep us safe?

96 How many taste buds are there on the tongue?

97 What are the five main tastes?

98 What are some of the sensations that sense receptions can pick up?

99 Name a part of the body with many sense receptors.

100 Where are smell receptor cells found?

101 Why is the sense of balance important?

102 What is proprioception?

WEIRD BODY FACTS

As well as being truly incredible, the human body is incredibly weird! Discover some disgusting and mind-blowing facts about different parts of the body.

In one year, we lose 4 kg of skin cells!

The epidermis is the outer layer of skin that we can see. New skin cells form at the bottom of the epidermis. They rise up to the surface and die when they get there, so our outer layer of skin is actually made up of dead skin cells! These dead cells eventually flake and fall off, and are replaced by new cells from underneath.

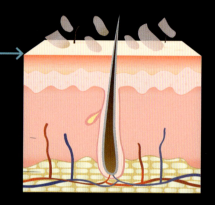

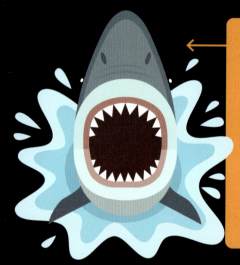

Human teeth are just as strong as shark teeth!

Both human and shark teeth are made up of tiny mineral crystals joined together with protein. This makes them equally strong! However, the difference in shape between human and shark teeth means that we eat in different ways. Shark teeth are pointed with jagged edges, which means that they can tear and saw through meat. Humans have different shapes of teeth for different purposes.

The human body contains the equivalent of over 40 teaspoons of salt!

The body contains many different salts, but the most common is sodium chloride, which is the salt that we eat on food. Our blood actually contains so much salt that it is roughly as salty as seawater! Although eating too much salt can cause health problems, such as high blood pressure, we need some salt in our diet to keep our blood and nerves healthy.

There are over 2 kg of microbes in the human body

Microbes are tiny living things, such as bacteria, viruses or fungi. There are a huge number of microbes in the human body, with ten microbes for every human cell! Together, these microbes are known as the microbiome. They help us to digest food in the large intestine, support the immune system and help to produce certain vitamins.

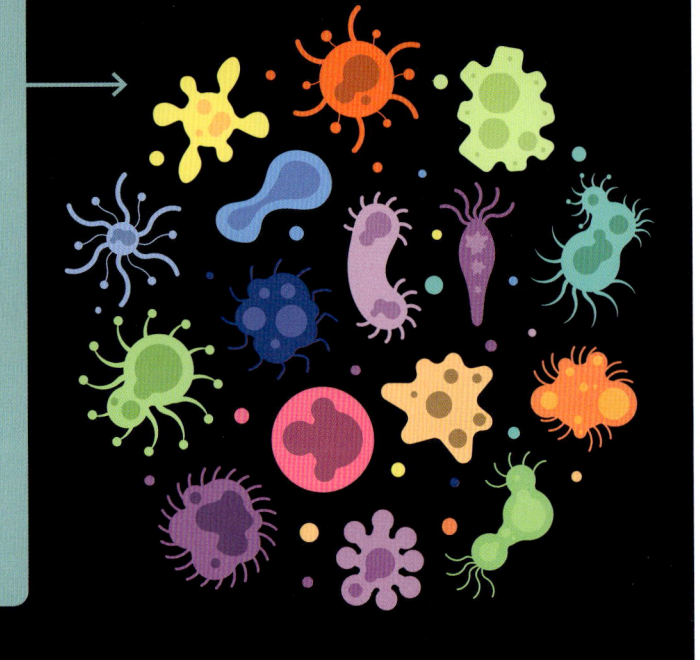

A sneeze leaves the body at speeds of up to 160 kph!

Sneezes are triggered when dust or chemicals irritate a nerve in the nose. First, we take a deep breath in. Then, a muscle in the chest called the diaphragm contracts, forcing air up and out through the nose, carrying mucus, dust and germs along with it! Droplets from a sneeze can travel up to 8 m, which is why it is important to cover your nose when you sneeze!

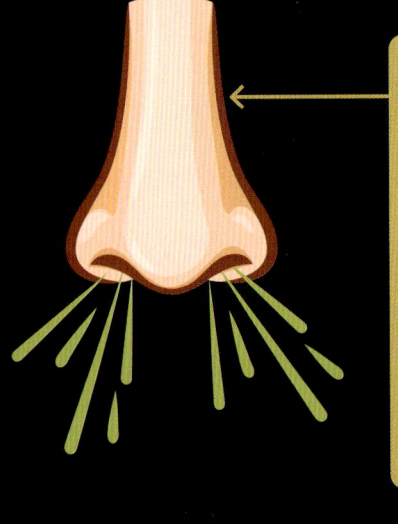

QUIZ TIME!

After you've finished testing yourself, why not use this book to make a quiz to test your friends and family? You could take questions from each section to make different rounds, or mix and match across the book for a general knowledge science quiz. You can even make up your own quiz questions! Use these weird and wonderful places facts to get you started. For example, '**What does the microbiome do?**' or '**How fast does a sneeze leave the body?**'

ANSWERS

1   An organ

2   Inside the chest and head

3   70 per cent

4   54.6 cm tall

5   5.6 m long

6   206

7   The femur (thigh bone)

8   The skull, spine and ribs

9   Compact bone

10 Red bone marrow

11 Skeletal, smooth and cardiac

12 Tendons

13 Up to 60 cm long

14 The eye

15 It relaxes

16 Smooth muscle

17 In the heart

18 The mouth, nose, windpipe and lungs

19 Waste gases, such as carbon dioxide

20 To create more space for air in the lungs

21 Around 30,000

22 A tiny air sac where gas exchange takes place

23 So that gases can pass through them

24 Between 8,000 and 9,000 litres

25 Around 2,414 km

26 17,000

27 The left side

28 The atrium and the ventricle

29 A blood vessel that carries blood from the heart to the body

30 A capillary

31 Carry oxygen around the body

32 Waste chemicals and hormones

33 Platelets

34 45 per cent

35 A nerve cell

36 Sensory neurone, motor neurone and relay neurone

37 The motor neurone

38 The brain and spinal cord

39 The neurones that stretch from the spinal cord to the toes

40 Up to 430 kph

41 Roughly 86 billion

42 Chemicals carry messages across the tiny gap between neurones

43 When the body reacts to something without receiving instructions from the brain

44 The cerebrum

45 The brainstem

46 Controls functions such as body temperature, sleep and hunger

47 The frontal lobe, the parietal lobe, the temporal lobe and the occipital lobe

48 To control memory and help us to understand language

49 The occipital lobe

50 Short-term memory and long-term memory

51 Because practising new tasks strengthens or makes new connections between neurones in the brain, making new tasks easier

52 Cutting, crushing and grinding food into smaller pieces

53 Around one litre

54 A flap that covers the windpipe

55 They push the food down towards the stomach

56 A thick liquid made up of broken-down food that is produced in the stomach

57 They contract to squeeze and churn the food to break it down

58 Around 0.5 to 1 mm long

59 The nutrients pass through blood vessels in the villi and into the bloodstream

60 9 m long

61 Water and some vitamins

62 Solid lumps of dried, undigested food

63 The rectum

64 To filter the blood and remove waste chemicals from it

65 10 cm long

66 Every 45 minutes

67 Tubes that carry urine from the kidneys to the bladder

68 Urine

69 The ovaries

70 Once a month

71 It remains in the womb until menstruation

72 The testicles

73 A child's body develops into the body of an adult and the reproductive system develops

74 The teenage years

75 Growing larger, voice becomes deeper, growing facial and pubic hair and hair in the armpits, chest and reproductive organs become larger

76 They get wider

77 The womb

78 40 weeks

79 Tiny hairs that trap the germs

80 Through cuts

81 They absorb germs and break them down into small, harmless pieces

82 Between 4,500 and 11,000

83 Chemicals that attack germs

84 So that the body learns how to makes the antibodies that fight the germ without actually becoming ill

85 Smallpox

86 Seeing, hearing, taste, touch and smell

87 The optic nerve

88 The retina

89 Cone cell

90 The eardrum

91 Tiny hairs pick up vibrations from the sound waves and convert them into a message that is sent to the brain

92 The earlobes

93 To keep dirt and germs out of the ear

94 Taste buds

95 It warns us against dangerous food such as rotten foods, that often taste bad

96 2,000 to 8,000

97 Sweet, salty, sour, bitter and umami

98 Hot or cold temperatures, different textures and pain

99 The fingertips

100 Inside the nose

101 It stops us from falling over

102 The sense of the position of the body and how it is moving

HOW WELL DID YOU DO?

100–102	- -> QUIZMASTER
75–99	- - - -> QUIZTASTIC
50–74	- - - - -> QUIZ ON
25–49	- - - - -> QUIZLING
0–24	- - - - -> QUIZ IT AGAIN

GLOSSARY

antibody – a chemical produced in the blood that attacks germs

blood vessel – a tube that carries blood

cell – a very small unit that all living things are made up of

chyme – a thick liquid made of broken-down food, found in the stomach

conscious – describes something that we are aware of

contract – to shrink

enzyme – a chemical that causes chemical reactions

filter – to remove something from something else

germ – a very small living thing that causes disease

hormone – a chemical made by the body that controls different processes

involuntary – not able to control

menstruation – the loss of the womb lining, resulting in a few days of bleeding every month

microbe – a very small living thing

mineral – a natural substance

mucus – a thick liquid produced in the nose and other parts of the body

neurone – a nerve cell

nutrient – a substance that humans or animals need to live and grow

organ – a body part with a particular function, such as the lungs

oxygen – a gas that cells in the body need to work properly

reflex reaction – an automatic reaction to something without receiving instructions from the brain

synapse – a gap between neurones that messages cross with the help of chemicals

tissue – a material made up of the same type of cells, such as bone or fat

vaccination – giving someone a weakened form of a germ to stop them from getting a disease

voluntary – able to control

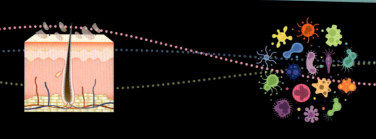

FURTHER INFORMATION

BOOKS

The Bright and Bold Human Body series
by Izzi Howell and Sonya Newland (Wayland, 2019)

Human Body (Infomojis)
by Jon Richards and Ed Simkins (Wayland, 2018)

Cause, Effect and Chaos in the Human Body
by Paul Mason (Wayland, 2018)

WEBSITES

www.dkfindout.com/uk/human-body/digestion/
Find out more about digestion and test your knowledge with a quiz.

www.bbc.co.uk/bitesize/topics/zwdr6yc/articles/zs8f8mn
Learn more about the circulatory system.

**ww.theguardian.com/childrens-books-site/gallery/2015/jan/25/
amazing-facts-you-didnt-know-about-the-human-body**
Discover some amazing facts about the human body.

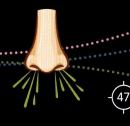

INDEX

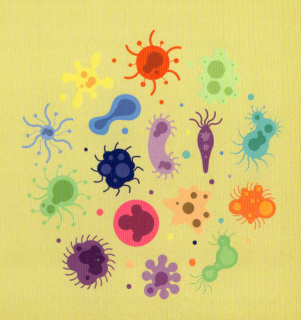